A History of the NFL

Gridiron Glory

By *Mike Bhangu*

Published by BB Productions

British Columbia, Canada

thinkingmanmike@gmail.com

A History of the NFL

Table of Contents

Introduction: Gridiron Glory

In the heart of America's sporting landscape, one institution stands as a beacon of athleticism, competition, and unbridled passion—the National Football League (NFL). From humble beginnings on sandlots and college fields to the grandeur of modern stadiums hosting the most-watched events in television history, the NFL's evolution is a story woven into the fabric of American culture.

"A History of the NFL: Gridiron Glory" invites you to embark on a riveting journey through the annals of the NFL, tracing the league's footsteps from its inception to the contemporary gridiron battles that captivate millions worldwide. This five-chapter odyssey unearths the tales of grit, strategy, triumph, and even heartbreak that have defined each era of the NFL's rich history.

In Chapter 1, we delve into the genesis of the league, exploring the audacious dreams of its founders, the challenges faced in the early days, and the birth of a competition that would capture the hearts of a nation.

Chapter 2 transports us to the dynamic Roaring Twenties, witnessing the rise of iconic teams and players. We navigate through the hardships of the Great Depression and the NFL's resilience, culminating in the merger with the AFL and the dawn of a new era.

The Golden Age unfolds in Chapter 3, where legendary coaches shape dynasties, televised broadcasts transform football into a national spectacle, and the Super Bowl becomes the pinnacle of American sports. The game evolves as strategies shift, and the league expands its reach both domestically and globally.

As we step into the Modern Era in Chapter 4, we witness the Steelers' steel curtain, the 49ers' West Coast brilliance, and the rise of individual football titans. The NFL becomes a 21st-century powerhouse, navigating challenges, embracing technology, and capturing hearts beyond borders.

Finally, in Chapter 5, we turn our gaze toward the present and future. From the impact of digital media to the ongoing quest for player safety, we explore the NFL's modern landscape. We examine the league's global expansion, the emergence of new stars, and the strides made in fostering diversity and inclusion.

"A History of the NFL: Gridiron Glory" is more than a chronicle; it's an invitation to relive the triumphs and tribulations that have shaped the NFL into a cultural phenomenon. Join us as we uncover the stories behind the touchdowns, the rivalries, and the moments that define the relentless pursuit of gridiron glory.

Chapter 1: Founding the League

Introduction to the Origins of American Football

The roots of American football can be traced back to the mid-19th century, a time when colleges and universities began to organize games that combined elements of soccer and rugby. The sport evolved gradually, with different regions adopting varying rules. The rough and tumble nature of these early contests captured the American spirit, reflecting the country's growing industrialization and toughness.

As the 19th century gave way to the 20th, a desire for a standardized set of rules and a professional league emerged. Football had become more than a collegiate pastime; it was evolving into a source of national pride and entertainment.

The Birth of the National Football League (NFL)

In 1920, the dream of a professional football league took a significant step forward with the establishment of the American Professional Football Association (APFA), which would later become the National Football League (NFL). Representatives from ten teams gathered in Canton, Ohio, to form the league, marking the birth of what would become the most popular and enduring professional football organization in the world.

Early Challenges and Rival Leagues

The NFL faced immediate challenges to its existence. Competing leagues, such as the Ohio League and the New York Pro Football League, vied for attention and talent. The NFL had to establish itself as the premier football league in the country, navigating the complexities of regional loyalties and rivalries.

Key Figures: Jim Thorpe, George Halas, and Others

Several visionary figures played pivotal roles in the establishment and early success of the NFL. Jim Thorpe, a multi-sport Olympic champion, became the league's first president. His charisma and athletic prowess lent credibility to the fledgling organization. George Halas, the founder and owner of the Chicago Bears, emerged as a central figure, contributing both on and off the field. These key figures brought legitimacy to the league, helping it gain traction in the eyes of the American public.

Formation of the First Teams and the Inaugural Season

The league's inaugural season in 1920 featured a mix of teams, including the Akron Pros, Canton Bulldogs, and Decatur Staleys (later renamed the Chicago Bears). These teams, comprised of players with diverse backgrounds and skill levels, laid the foundation for the professional football we know today.

The inaugural season showcased the league's commitment to competition and entertainment. Games were played on makeshift fields, often in front of modest crowds, but the passion and determination of the players were undeniable.

Milestones and Challenges During the Early Years

The early years of the NFL were marked by both milestones and challenges. The league expanded, welcoming new teams and facing the complexities of scheduling and travel. The 1922 season witnessed the first tiebreaker game, a precursor to modern playoff formats. Financial struggles, however, were a constant companion, with several teams folding due to economic hardships.

The NFL's perseverance through these challenges signaled its resilience and determination to establish itself as a lasting institution. The league's early years laid the groundwork for the exciting and unpredictable future that awaited, as the NFL embarked on a journey that would see it evolve into the iconic American institution we know today.

Expansion and Evolution

As the NFL navigated the challenges of its early years, the league underwent significant expansion. New teams, each with its unique identity, joined the ranks, contributing to the league's growing tapestry. Cities such as Green Bay, Detroit, and New York became synonymous with the passion and excitement of professional football.

The evolution of the game itself was evident as teams experimented with different strategies, and the rules underwent refinements to enhance the overall experience for players and fans alike. The commitment to innovation was a testament to the NFL's determination to provide a dynamic and compelling product.

Key Figures Leave Indelible Marks

Jim Thorpe's tenure as the league's first president set a precedent for leadership. His dedication to the game and vision for a professional league paved the way for subsequent leaders who would carry the torch forward. George Halas, with his visionary approach, not only established the Chicago Bears as a football powerhouse but also became an influential force in shaping the league's direction.

Other key figures, such as Art Rooney and Tim Mara, demonstrated a commitment to their respective teams and communities, fostering a sense of belonging that would become a hallmark of the NFL. These early architects laid the groundwork for the league's enduring connection with fans and its integral role in American culture.

Competing Visions and the NFL's Resilience

Despite the challenges posed by rival leagues and economic uncertainties, the NFL's resilience shone through. The league weathered storms and faced the prospect of extinction during the Depression era. The perseverance of team owners, players, and supporters became a defining feature of the NFL's character.

While rival leagues folded or merged, the NFL stood its ground, steadily building a foundation that would elevate it beyond a regional attraction. The challenges of the early years became stepping stones, fueling the league's determination to become a national institution.

Legacy of the Inaugural Season

The inaugural season of the NFL left an indelible mark on the American sports landscape. It showcased the potential of professional football, even in the face of adversity. The passion of players and fans, combined with the strategic vision of league leaders, forged a legacy that transcended the uncertainties of the time.

As the league moved forward, it carried with it the spirit of the inaugural season—the belief that football could capture the imagination of a nation and unite communities. The milestones achieved and challenges overcome during these formative years became the building blocks for a future filled with iconic moments, legendary players, and a cultural phenomenon that would extend far beyond the gridiron.

Conclusion of Chapter 1

The founding of the NFL was not just the establishment of a sports league; it was the planting of a seed that would grow into a mighty oak, casting its shadow over American culture for generations to come. The challenges faced, the key figures who emerged, and the milestones achieved during these early years laid the foundation for the NFL's ascent to greatness. As we move forward in this journey through the annals of football history, the echoes of the inaugural season continue to resonate, reminding us of the league's humble origins and the relentless pursuit of gridiron glory.

Chapter 2: The Roaring Twenties to the NFL-AFL Merger

The Impact of the Roaring Twenties on the NFL

The Roaring Twenties, a period of economic prosperity and cultural dynamism, left an indelible mark on the National Football League (NFL). As the nation embraced a newfound sense of optimism and exuberance, the NFL underwent transformative changes, evolving from a regional pastime into a national spectacle.

The 1920s witnessed an explosion of interest in professional football. The NFL, once a collection of regional teams, began to capture the imagination of fans across the country. The league's popularity soared as star players emerged, showcasing their athletic prowess and contributing to the creation of football icons. Teams like the Chicago Bears, Green Bay Packers, and New York Giants became symbols of a burgeoning sporting culture.

Rise of Star Players and Iconic Teams

The Roaring Twenties were a crucible for the forging of football legends. Players like Red Grange, the "Galloping Ghost," captured the nation's attention with his electrifying performances. Grange's signing with the Chicago Bears in 1925 marked a turning point, as his star power drew unprecedented crowds and media attention. The era saw the rise of iconic teams, each with its unique style and charismatic players, adding to the allure of professional football.

The Packers, under the leadership of Curly Lambeau, began to establish themselves as a football powerhouse, laying the groundwork for their future dominance. Meanwhile, the Giants, led by innovative coach Steve Owen, became known for their rugged style of play, embodying the spirit of a rapidly changing America.

The Great Depression and its Impact on the League

The economic devastation wrought by the Great Depression cast a shadow over the NFL in the early 1930s. Attendance dwindled, and several teams faced financial hardships. Franchises folded, and the league experienced a contraction as it grappled with the harsh economic realities of the time.

However, even in the face of adversity, the NFL demonstrated resilience. The survival of teams like the Green Bay Packers, owned by the community, exemplified the league's ability to weather economic storms. As the nation emerged from the Depression, the NFL, like the country itself, found renewed vigor and optimism.

Innovations in Gameplay and Strategy

Amidst economic challenges, the NFL witnessed innovations in gameplay and strategy that laid the foundation for the modern era. Coaches like George Halas and Clark Shaughnessy introduced new offensive and defensive schemes, forever altering the way the game was played.

The introduction of the T-formation revolutionized offensive strategy, allowing for more intricate plays and emphasizing the forward pass. This shift in tactics transformed football into a more dynamic and strategic sport, captivating audiences with its unpredictability.

NFL during World War II

As World War II engulfed the globe, the NFL faced challenges akin to those experienced during the Great Depression. Player rosters were depleted as many athletes joined the war effort. The league, however, continued to provide a sense of normalcy and entertainment to a nation in turmoil.

War-time rosters featured a mix of seasoned veterans and replacement players, showcasing the league's adaptability. The Cleveland Rams temporarily suspended operations, symbolizing the war's impact on professional sports. Despite these challenges, the NFL soldiered on, becoming a source of inspiration and unity during difficult times.

The All-America Football Conference (AAFC) and its Merger with the NFL

In the post-war period, a new challenge emerged in the form of the All-America Football Conference (AAFC), a rival league that sought to compete with the NFL. Established in 1946, the AAFC featured teams in major cities and introduced innovations such as the concept of the face mask.

The competition between the NFL and AAFC was fierce, with both leagues vying for talent and fan support. The Cleveland Browns, led by coach Paul Brown and quarterback Otto Graham, emerged as the AAFC's dominant force, winning multiple championships.

In 1950, recognizing the benefits of unity, the NFL and AAFC merged. The Cleveland Browns, San Francisco 49ers, and Baltimore Colts joined the NFL, enriching the league with new talent and perspectives. The merger marked a transformative moment, solidifying the NFL's status as the premier professional football league in the United States.

The Roaring Twenties, the challenges of the Great Depression, the innovations of gameplay and strategy, the resilience of the NFL during World War II, and the merger with the AAFC—all these elements defined a pivotal era in the league's history. As we move forward, the NFL stands at the crossroads of a changing sports landscape, ready to face new challenges and continue its journey toward gridiron glory.

Era of Dominance and Innovation

As the NFL emerged from the challenges of the Great Depression and World War II, a new era unfolded, characterized by dominance and innovation. The post-war period witnessed a surge in popularity, and the league's expansion and integration of AAFC teams added a layer of competitiveness that fueled excitement among fans.

Teams like the Cleveland Browns seamlessly transitioned from the AAFC to the NFL, maintaining their winning tradition. Led by the visionary coach Paul Brown and quarterback Otto Graham, the Browns became a force to be reckoned with, setting the stage for an era of unprecedented success.

Innovation continued to be a driving force in the NFL's evolution. The 1950s saw the advent of televised games, bringing football into the living rooms of millions. This technological leap transformed the league into a national spectacle, amplifying its reach and solidifying its status as America's favorite sport.

Chapter 3: The Golden Age of the NFL: 1950s-1960s

Emergence of Legendary Coaches - Vince Lombardi, Paul Brown, and Others

The 1950s and 1960s are often hailed as the Golden Age of the NFL, marked by the emergence of legendary coaches who left an indelible mark on the league. Chief among them was Vince Lombardi, the stoic leader of the Green Bay Packers. Lombardi's meticulous attention to detail and unwavering commitment to excellence transformed the Packers into a football dynasty, earning him a legacy that transcends generations.

Paul Brown, the innovative mind behind the Cleveland Browns, also played a pivotal role in shaping the era. Brown's forward-thinking approach to the game laid the foundation for modern coaching techniques, emphasizing precision and strategic planning.

Other coaching luminaries, including Tom Landry of the Dallas Cowboys and George Halas of the Chicago Bears, contributed to the league's rich tapestry. These coaches not only led their teams to success but also became iconic figures synonymous with the greatness of the NFL.

The Advent of Televised Games and the Rise of Football as a National Spectacle

The 1950s witnessed a transformative moment in sports history—the advent of televised NFL games. This technological leap brought football into the living rooms of millions of Americans, forever changing the way the sport was consumed. The medium of television turned the NFL into a national spectacle, captivating audiences with the drama, intensity, and camaraderie of the game.

As families gathered around their television sets, the NFL became more than a sport; it became a shared cultural experience. Iconic moments, thrilling plays, and the sheer excitement of football contributed to the rise of the NFL as an integral part of American life.

Expansion of the League and Introduction of New Teams

The popularity of televised games fueled the expansion of the NFL. New teams were introduced, representing cities across the country and broadening the league's reach. The Baltimore Colts, Minnesota Vikings, and Atlanta Falcons were among the franchises added during this period, each contributing to the diversity and competitiveness of the NFL.

The league's expansion was a reflection of its growing stature, as more fans embraced the sport, and the NFL solidified its position as the preeminent professional football league.

The Iconic Rivalry Between the Green Bay Packers and the Dallas Cowboys

The 1960s witnessed the birth of an iconic rivalry that would define the era—the Green Bay Packers versus the Dallas Cowboys. These two powerhouse teams clashed in epic battles, creating a narrative of competition, sportsmanship, and unforgettable moments.

The Packers, led by Vince Lombardi, and the Cowboys, under the guidance of Tom Landry, engaged in a series of playoff showdowns that became the stuff of legends. The "Ice Bowl" in 1967, played in frigid conditions at Lambeau Field, stands as a testament to the intensity and drama of this rivalry.

Super Bowl Era Begins: The First Super Bowl and the Merger with the AFL

The pinnacle of the NFL season underwent a transformative shift in the 1960s with the inception of the Super Bowl. The champions of the NFL and the American Football League (AFL) faced off in a spectacle that transcended traditional championship games. The first Super Bowl, played in 1967, saw the Green Bay Packers defeat the Kansas City Chiefs, marking the beginning of an annual tradition that would capture the world's imagination.

The late 1960s also saw the merger of the NFL and AFL, uniting the two rival leagues into a single entity. The merger not only expanded the league but also set the stage for a new era of competition, collaboration, and the establishment of the NFL as the undisputed leader in professional football.

Evolution of the Game: From Running to Passing Dominance

The 1950s and 1960s witnessed a significant evolution in the style of play, transitioning from a run-heavy game to one dominated by passing.

Quarterbacks like Johnny Unitas, Bart Starr, and Joe Namath emerged as stars, showcasing precision passing and strategic brilliance.

Innovations in offensive strategies, such as the West Coast Offense, further emphasized the passing game. The "Air Coryell" system, implemented by the San Diego Chargers, showcased the potential of a high-flying, pass-centric approach. This shift in tactics not only led to more exciting and dynamic gameplay but also set the stage for the quarterback-centric league we see today.

The Golden Age of the NFL, spanning the 1950s and 1960s, was a period of profound transformation and enduring legacy. Legendary coaches, the advent of televised games, the expansion of the league, iconic rivalries, the birth of the Super Bowl, and the evolution of the game itself—these elements combined to create a foundation for the NFL's continued ascent toward gridiron glory.

The Legacy of Legendary Coaches

Vince Lombardi, often referred to as the namesake of the Super Bowl trophy, became synonymous with leadership, discipline, and excellence. His tenure with the Green Bay Packers saw the team secure five NFL championships and two Super Bowl victories. Lombardi's impact extended beyond the field, as his coaching philosophy became a blueprint for success in the NFL.

Paul Brown, a pioneer in football coaching, not only founded the Cleveland Browns but also introduced innovative approaches to scouting, film analysis, and play-calling. His legacy endured not only through his coaching achievements but also through the numerous coaching disciples he mentored, who went on to shape the future of the NFL.

Televised Games and the National Spectacle

The introduction of televised games in the 1950s was a game-changer, turning football into a national phenomenon. Families across the nation gathered on Sunday afternoons to witness the drama unfold on their screens. The iconic voice of announcer John Facenda and the visual spectacle of the games created an indelible image of the NFL in the hearts of fans.

Television not only brought the game to the fans but also allowed the NFL to showcase its stars, enhancing the connection between players and the audience. The rise of football as a televised sport laid the foundation for the multi-billion-dollar broadcasting contracts that would later become a cornerstone of the league's financial success.

Expansion and New Teams

The expansion of the NFL in the 1960s marked a period of geographic diversification. New franchises brought the excitement of professional football to previously untapped markets. The Baltimore Colts, led by Johnny Unitas, became a powerhouse in the league. The Minnesota Vikings and Atlanta Falcons added their unique identities to the growing landscape of the NFL.

This expansion not only broadened the league's fanbase but also intensified competition, leading to a more dynamic and unpredictable NFL. The addition of these teams contributed to the rich tapestry of the league, creating new rivalries and enhancing the overall drama of the game.

Iconic Rivalry - Green Bay Packers vs. Dallas Cowboys

The rivalry between the Green Bay Packers and the Dallas Cowboys became a defining narrative of the 1960s. These two teams clashed in epic battles, particularly in the NFL Championship games and playoffs. The Ice Bowl, played in sub-zero temperatures at Lambeau Field in 1967, remains one of the most memorable moments in NFL history.

Led by coaches Vince Lombardi and Tom Landry, and featuring iconic players like Bart Starr and Roger Staubach, these matchups captivated audiences and contributed to the lore of the NFL. The Packers and Cowboys rivalry showcased the intensity and sportsmanship that define the spirit of the game.

Super Bowl Era and the Merger with the AFL

The inaugural Super Bowl in 1967 between the Green Bay Packers and the Kansas City Chiefs marked the beginning of a new era. The merger with the American Football League (AFL) in 1970 not only expanded the league but also paved the way for a unified championship game that would captivate the world.

The merger was a strategic move that allowed the NFL to consolidate talent, reduce competition, and create a more compelling product for fans. The first few Super Bowls showcased the dominance of NFL teams, but over time, the merger led to greater parity between the two leagues, enhancing the overall quality of competition.

Evolution of the Game - Passing Dominance

The 1950s and 1960s saw a transformative shift in offensive strategies, with a move towards passing dominance. Quarterbacks like Johnny Unitas, Bart Starr, and Joe Namath became stars, showcasing precision passing and strategic brilliance. The West Coast Offense, popularized by Bill Walsh, emphasized short, accurate passes and changed the dynamics of offensive play.

This shift laid the groundwork for the modern passing game, where quarterbacks and their aerial assaults became focal points of team strategies. The NFL's evolution during this period set the stage for the high-scoring, pass-heavy games that define the league today.

The Golden Age of the NFL in the 1950s and 1960s was a time of innovation, growth, and the establishment of enduring legacies. Legendary coaches, televised games, league expansion, iconic rivalries, the birth of the Super Bowl, and the evolution of offensive strategies—all these elements contributed to shaping the NFL into the cultural and sporting juggernaut it is today. As the league moved forward, it carried the lessons and triumphs of this golden era into a future filled with continued gridiron glory.

The Cultural Impact of Legendary Coaches

The influence of legendary coaches like Vince Lombardi and Paul Brown extended far beyond the football field. Lombardi's leadership style, marked by discipline, dedication, and a commitment to fundamentals, became a blueprint for success not only in football but in various fields. His famous axiom, "Winning isn't everything; it's the only thing," resonated in the hearts of competitors and enthusiasts alike.

Paul Brown's contributions were equally profound. His innovations in scouting, play-calling, and personnel management laid the groundwork for modern coaching methods. The coaching tree that sprouted from Brown's teachings included luminaries like Bill Walsh, Chuck Noll, and Don Shula, who, in turn, left their own indelible marks on the NFL.

Televised Games - Transforming Football into a National Obsession

Television transformed football from a regional pastime into a national obsession. The iconic voices of commentators like Howard Cosell and the visual spectacle of the games became cultural touchstones. Families and friends gathered around television sets, creating a communal experience that transcended demographics.

The advent of color television added another layer to the viewing experience, bringing the vibrant colors of team uniforms and the lush green of the field to living rooms across America. The NFL's partnership with television networks laid the foundation for the league's economic prosperity and global reach.

Expansion and New Teams - A Growing Tapestry of the NFL

The addition of new teams during the 1960s not only expanded the NFL geographically but also introduced fresh narratives and rivalries. The Baltimore Colts became a powerhouse in the league, with Johnny Unitas at the helm. The Minnesota Vikings brought a rugged, defensive identity to the league, while the Atlanta Falcons added a Southern flair.

This period of expansion showcased the NFL's adaptability and foresight. The league's willingness to embrace new markets broadened its appeal, and the addition of these teams enriched the tapestry of the NFL, creating diverse fanbases and intensifying competition.

Legacy and Beyond

The Golden Age of the NFL in the 1950s and 1960s left an enduring legacy. The cultural impact of legendary coaches, the transformative power of televised games, the expansion of the league, iconic rivalries, the birth of the Super Bowl, and the evolution of offensive strategies— these elements shaped the NFL into the cultural juggernaut it is today.

As the league moved forward, it carried the spirit of this golden era, mindful of the lessons learned and the traditions established. The Golden Age not only solidified the NFL's position in American sports culture but also set the stage for decades of gridiron glory, showcasing the resilience, innovation, and enduring appeal of professional football.

Chapter 4: The Modern Era: 1970s-2000s

The Dominance of Powerhouse Teams - Pittsburgh Steelers and San Francisco 49ers

The Modern Era of the NFL, spanning the 1970s to the 2000s, witnessed the emergence of powerhouse teams that left an indelible mark on the league. Chief among them were the Pittsburgh Steelers and the San Francisco 49ers, each defining their own era of dominance.

The Pittsburgh Steelers, led by the iconic "Steel Curtain" defense and quarterback Terry Bradshaw, secured four Super Bowl championships in the 1970s. Coached by Chuck Noll, the Steelers became synonymous with a physical and relentless style of play, leaving an enduring legacy as one of the greatest dynasties in NFL history.

The San Francisco 49ers, under the guidance of innovative coach Bill Walsh, ushered in the West Coast Offense era. Quarterback Joe Montana, along with a cast of talented players, including wide receiver Jerry Rice, became the faces of a team that secured five Super Bowl victories during the 1980s. The 49ers' precision passing and strategic brilliance set new standards for offensive excellence.

The Impact of Rule Changes and Technological Advancements

The Modern Era was marked by significant rule changes and technological advancements that shaped the way the game was played. Rule changes, such as those aimed at enhancing player safety and encouraging passing offenses, transformed the dynamics of play on the field.

Technological innovations, including the advent of instant replay and advancements in sports science and analytics, provided teams with new tools for evaluating performance and making strategic decisions. The integration of technology not only improved the accuracy of officiating but also revolutionized the way teams approached player development and game planning.

Emergence of Superstar Players - Joe Montana, Jerry Rice, Walter Payton, and Others

The Modern Era introduced a pantheon of superstar players whose individual brilliance contributed to the league's allure. Joe Montana, often heralded as one of the greatest quarterbacks of all time, crafted a legacy defined by clutch performances and four Super Bowl victories.

Jerry Rice, widely regarded as the greatest wide receiver in NFL history, rewrote the record books and set standards for excellence that are yet to be surpassed. His partnership with Joe Montana and later Steve Young formed the backbone of the San Francisco 49ers' offensive prowess.

Walter Payton, the iconic running back of the Chicago Bears, became a symbol of durability, versatility, and sportsmanship. His record-breaking career and Super Bowl victory in 1985 solidified his status as one of the game's all-time greats.

The Modern Era also witnessed the rise of other legendary players, including quarterbacks like Dan Marino, running backs like Emmitt Smith, and defensive stalwarts like Lawrence Taylor, each leaving an indelible mark on the league.

Expansion and Realignment of the League

The NFL underwent significant expansion and realignment during the Modern Era. New teams were added, including the Jacksonville Jaguars, Carolina Panthers, and later the Houston Texans, bringing the total number of franchises to 32. This expansion not only broadened the league's geographic footprint but also facilitated the creation of new rivalries.

Realignment of divisions aimed to ensure competitive balance and foster regional rivalries. Changes to the playoff format also occurred, further intensifying competition and creating a more dynamic postseason landscape.

The Rise of the Dallas Cowboys and the Dynasty of the New England Patriots

The Dallas Cowboys, under the leadership of owner Jerry Jones and coach Jimmy Johnson, experienced a resurgence in the 1990s. A roster featuring talents like Troy Aikman, Emmitt Smith, and Michael Irvin propelled the Cowboys to three Super Bowl victories in a span of four years, solidifying their status as a dominant force in the league.

In the 2000s, the New England Patriots, led by coach Bill Belichick and quarterback Tom Brady, embarked on a historic dynasty. The Patriots secured six Super Bowl victories, establishing themselves as the preeminent team of the era. The combination of strategic brilliance, disciplined execution, and a relentless pursuit of excellence made the Patriots a model franchise.

The NFL's Globalization and the Growth of International Interest

The Modern Era saw the NFL evolve into a global phenomenon, with concerted efforts to expand its reach beyond American borders. International games became an annual occurrence, with matchups held in London and Mexico City, fostering a global fanbase and sparking interest in American football on a worldwide scale.

The league's commitment to international growth extended beyond games, with initiatives such as the NFL International Series and partnerships with international organizations. The Super Bowl, already a global event, became a showcase for the league's international ambitions, attracting viewers from every corner of the globe.

The Evolution of Playing Styles

During the Modern Era, the NFL witnessed an evolution in playing styles. The dominance of pass-oriented offenses became increasingly prevalent, with quarterbacks assuming central roles as field generals. The West Coast Offense, popularized by Bill Walsh and refined by subsequent coaches, continued to influence offensive strategies across the league.

Innovation extended to defensive schemes as well, with the rise of complex formations and versatile players capable of disrupting passing lanes and pressuring quarterbacks. The balance between high-scoring offenses and formidable defenses became a defining characteristic of the era.

Super Bowl Moments and Memorable Games

The Super Bowl continued to captivate audiences with memorable moments and iconic matchups. Super Bowl XXV, where the New York Giants thwarted the high-powered Buffalo Bills in a nail-biting 20-19 victory, showcased the strategic prowess of both teams and the importance of every play in championship contests.

Super Bowl XXXVI marked the beginning of the New England Patriots' dynasty as they defeated the heavily favored St. Louis Rams. The game featured a last-second game-winning field goal by Adam Vinatieri, setting the stage for the Patriots' unprecedented success in the early 2000s.

The Emergence of Quarterback Dynasties

The Modern Era solidified the quarterback position as the focal point of success in the NFL. Quarterback dynasties, led by legendary figures like Joe Montana, Troy Aikman, and Tom Brady, became emblematic of their respective teams' sustained success.

Joe Montana's unrivaled poise in clutch moments earned him the nickname "Joe Cool," and his four Super Bowl victories with the San Francisco 49ers remain a benchmark for quarterback excellence. Troy

Aikman's leadership guided the Dallas Cowboys to three Super Bowl titles in the 1990s, cementing his legacy as one of the franchise's greatest quarterbacks.

Tom Brady's ascent to stardom with the New England Patriots marked a new era of quarterback dominance. His partnership with coach Bill Belichick resulted in six Super Bowl victories, making Brady synonymous with championship success and rewriting the record books.

The Impact of Free Agency and Salary Cap

The implementation of free agency and a salary cap in the 1990s transformed the landscape of player movement and team-building. Players gained more control over their careers, and teams were forced to navigate the delicate balance of maintaining competitiveness while managing financial constraints.

This era saw the rise of player movement, with marquee free-agent signings altering the trajectories of franchises. The salary cap, designed to promote parity, contributed to an environment where every team had a realistic chance of success, further intensifying competition.

Unforgettable Performances and Records

The Modern Era witnessed remarkable individual performances that etched players into the annals of NFL history. Emmitt Smith's career rushing record, surpassing Walter Payton, exemplified sustained excellence. Jerry Rice's enduring brilliance in the passing game set records that seemed insurmountable.

Additionally, record-setting passing performances became commonplace, with quarterbacks like Dan Marino, Peyton Manning, and Brett Favre shattering long-standing records for passing yards and touchdowns. These achievements added a layer of individual excellence to the broader narrative of team success.

Chapter Conclusion

As the NFL navigated the complexities of the Modern Era, it weaved a tapestry of excellence marked by dominant teams, iconic players, strategic innovations, and a growing global footprint. The era set the stage for a new millennium where the league's popularity soared to unprecedented heights, capturing the imaginations of fans worldwide.

The NFL's ability to adapt to changing dynamics, embrace technological advancements, and showcase the talents of extraordinary athletes solidified its status as a cultural force. The Modern Era laid the groundwork for a future where the pursuit of gridiron glory would continue to evolve, fueled by the passion of fans and the indomitable spirit of competition.

Chapter 5: The 21st Century and Beyond

The Impact of Digital Media on the NFL

The 21st century ushered in a digital revolution that transformed the way fans engage with the NFL. The advent of digital media, streaming platforms, and social media significantly expanded the league's reach and accessibility. Fans could now consume games, highlights, and exclusive content on various digital platforms, fostering a global community of football enthusiasts.

The NFL capitalized on this shift, launching official apps, streaming services, and social media accounts to connect with fans in real-time. Digital media not only provided a new avenue for fan engagement but also became a crucial component of the league's marketing and revenue-generation strategies.

Challenges and Controversies - Player Safety, Concussions, and Social Issues

The 21st century brought forth a heightened awareness of player safety, with a specific focus on the long-term effects of concussions. The NFL faced scrutiny and legal challenges regarding its handling of head injuries, leading to increased efforts to improve player safety protocols, rule changes, and advancements in helmet technology.

Moreover, the league grappled with controversies surrounding social issues, including player protests during the national anthem to raise awareness about racial injustice. These incidents sparked intense public discourse and prompted the NFL to navigate the delicate balance between addressing societal concerns and maintaining its traditional image.

Expansion of the League with New Franchises

The NFL continued its expansion efforts in the 21st century, adding new franchises to its roster. The Houston Texans joined the league in 2002 as the 32nd team, bringing professional football back to the state of Texas. The addition of the Texans not only expanded the league's footprint but also contributed to the growing popularity of the sport in non-traditional football markets.

The success of international games and the increasing global interest in the NFL led to discussions about the possibility of adding franchises outside the United States, further illustrating the league's commitment to its global fanbase.

Emergence of New Stars - Tom Brady, Peyton Manning, and Others

The 21st century witnessed the emergence of new gridiron legends who would leave an indelible mark on the NFL. Tom Brady, the quarterback synonymous with the New England Patriots, became a symbol of sustained excellence and championship success. His leadership and unparalleled success in Super Bowls solidified his status as one of the greatest quarterbacks in NFL history.

Peyton Manning, known for his football IQ and prolific passing, set numerous records throughout his career, including the most touchdown passes in a single season. Manning's impact extended beyond the field, shaping the quarterback position and influencing a generation of players.

A new generation of stars, including Patrick Mahomes, Lamar Jackson, and Aaron Donald, continued to captivate audiences with their exceptional talents, ensuring a seamless transition of star power into the future.

The Role of Fantasy Football and Sports Betting

Fantasy football and sports betting emerged as cultural phenomena that further enriched the NFL experience. Fantasy football, with its drafting, team management, and weekly matchups, turned fans into virtual team owners, fostering a deeper connection to the league and individual players.

Sports betting, once a taboo topic in American sports, gained acceptance and became intertwined with the NFL's narrative. The league embraced partnerships with sportsbook operators, acknowledging the role of sports betting in enhancing fan engagement while maintaining the integrity of the game.

Fan Engagement - The Heartbeat of the NFL's Future

At the core of the NFL's enduring success is the unwavering support of its fans. As the league progresses into the future, fan engagement remains a central focus. The NFL recognizes the importance of fostering a deep and meaningful connection with its diverse and passionate audience.

Digital platforms, social media, and interactive experiences are key components in this endeavor. The NFL's continued investment in technology aims to create personalized and immersive experiences that resonate with fans of all ages. From virtual reality tailgates to interactive game-day apps, the league seeks to bring the excitement of NFL football directly to the fingertips of fans around the globe.

The NFL's Efforts in Promoting Diversity and Inclusion

The 21st century marked a concerted effort by the NFL to promote diversity and inclusion within the league and its fanbase. Initiatives such as the Rooney Rule aimed to increase diversity in coaching and executive positions. The league also expanded its commitment to social justice causes, fostering partnerships with players and organizations dedicated to addressing systemic issues.

The NFL recognized the power of its platform to drive positive change and became more actively involved in community outreach programs, philanthropy, and initiatives promoting equality and inclusion.

The Future of the NFL - Innovations, Challenges, and the Continuing Legacy of America's Favorite Sport

Looking ahead, the NFL faces a future defined by both innovation and challenges. Technological advancements, including augmented reality, virtual reality, and enhanced viewing experiences, promise to elevate the fan experience. The continued global expansion of the league and potential franchise additions outside the United States could further solidify the NFL as a truly international sport.

However, challenges persist, including ongoing concerns about player safety, evolving societal expectations, and the ever-changing media landscape. Navigating these challenges will require adaptability and a commitment to maintaining the integrity and appeal of the sport.

As the NFL progresses into the future, it does so with a legacy built on the shoulders of its storied past. The enduring passion of fans, the remarkable talents of players, and the league's ability to evolve with the times ensure that American football will continue to hold a special place in the hearts of millions, securing its position as America's favorite sport for generations to come.

Chapter Conclusion

As the NFL steps boldly into the 21st century and beyond, it does so with a tapestry richly woven from the threads of tradition, innovation, and resilience. The league's legacy, built over decades of thrilling competition, cultural impact, and societal relevance, serves as a foundation for the chapters yet to be written.

The NFL's future promises a dynamic interplay of tradition and progress, as it embraces new technologies, addresses societal challenges, and expands its global footprint. The heartbeat of the league remains its fans, whose unwavering passion and dedication ensure that the spirit of gridiron glory will continue to echo across stadiums, living rooms, and communities for generations to come.

As the NFL's narrative unfolds, one thing remains certain: America's favorite sport will continue to captivate hearts, inspire dreams, and stand as a symbol of unity, competition, and the enduring spirit of a nation. The journey continues, and the best may still be yet to come.

Conclusion: Unveiling the Legacy of the NFL

As the final whistle echoes through the pages of "A History of the NFL: Gridiron Glory," we find ourselves standing at the end zone of a journey that has traversed the epochs of the National Football League (NFL). The history of the NFL is not merely a collection of wins and losses, but a mosaic of tales woven into the cultural fabric of American life.

From the ambitious dreams of its founders in Chapter 1 to the grandeur of the modern gridiron battles explored in Chapter 5, this chronicle has painted a vivid portrait of a league that evolved from humble beginnings into a cultural phenomenon. Each chapter unfurled a new layer of the NFL's narrative, revealing the resilience, passion, and innovation that have defined its journey.

In the early days, pioneers dared to dream of a league that would capture the hearts of a nation. The Roaring Twenties brought us the icons, the Great Depression tested the league's mettle, and the merger with the AFL in the 1960s marked a transformative moment that ushered in a new era of football.

The Golden Age, with its legendary coaches and televised spectacles, catapulted the NFL into the hearts of millions. It was an era where the Super Bowl became the grand stage for football immortality, and the game evolved in tandem with the cultural landscape.

The Modern Era, with its technological innovations, global expansion, and individual brilliance, saw the NFL cement its status as a 21st-century powerhouse. This era also brought forth challenges—concussions, player safety, and controversies—that forced the league to adapt and evolve.

As we stand in the present, Chapter 5 has peeled back the layers of the NFL's contemporary landscape. The league has embraced digital media, expanded globally, and championed diversity and inclusion. It's a testament to the NFL's adaptability and its commitment to remaining a cornerstone of American sports.

"A History of the NFL: Gridiron Glory" has sought to celebrate the triumphs and acknowledge the challenges that have defined the NFL. As we conclude this journey, we recognize that the legacy of the NFL is not confined to statistics or championship titles. It lives in the roar of the crowd, the grit of the players, and the indomitable spirit that has fueled the passion for football across generations.

The NFL's story is ongoing, with new chapters yet to be written. "A History of the NFL: Gridiron Glory" has been our guide through the annals of history, a tribute to the enduring legacy of a league that transcends sport to become a cultural touchstone. As the echoes of gridiron battles fade, we carry with us the tales of triumph, the lessons of adversity, and the indelible mark left by those who dared to chase gridiron glory.

Printed in Great Britain
by Amazon